GOD'S LITTLE

★ INSTRUCTION BOOK ★

FOR THE CLASS OF

2014

GOD'S LITTLE

★ INSTRUCTION BOOK ★

FOR THE CLASS OF

2014

David C Cook

transforming lives together

GOD'S LITTLE INSTRUCTION BOOK FOR THE CLASS OF 2014
David C Cook
4050 Lee Vance View
Colorado Springs, CO 80918 U.S.A.

David C Cook Distribution Canada
55 Woodslee Avenue, Paris, Ontario, Canada N3L 3E5

David C Cook U.K., Kingsway Communications
Eastbourne, East Sussex BN23 6NT, England

The graphic circle C logo is a registered trademark of David C Cook.

Bible credits are located at the end of this book.

ISBN 978-1-4347-0742-0

© 2014 David C Cook

The Team: Ingrid Beck, Amy Konyndyk, Tonya Osterhouse, Karen Athen
Cover and Interior Design: Nick Lee

Printed in the United States of America

First Edition 2014
1 2 3 4 5 6 7 8 9 10

010314

INTRODUCTION

Congratulations! As a member of the Class of 2014, you are part of a new and changing millennium filled with innovative technologies and amazing discoveries.

These exciting times have made the earth a much more challenging and complicated place to live. You will be confronted with opportunities to make wise decisions and to be a shining light in an often dark and confusing place. How do you make good choices when everything around you is moving and changing? And how do you cut through the hype and find what is good?

In *God's Little Instruction Book for the Class of 2014,* we offer you wisdom sufficient to help you navigate the twenty-first century. We have taken quotes from ordinary people and heroes throughout history and combined them with wisdom from the Bible to help you become the person you aspire to be. We hope the truths presented in these pages will help you settle your life on an unshakable foundation and enable you to build a world filled with infinite possibilities.

The world wants your best, but God wants your all.

—*Author unknown*

Thou shalt love the Lord thy God with all thy heart, and with all thy soul, and with all thy mind.

Matthew 22:37 KJV

FOR THE CLASS OF
2014

GOD'S LITTLE

★ **INSTRUCTION BOOK** ★

The future is as bright as the promises of God.

—William Carey

Whatever God has promised gets stamped with the Yes of Jesus.

2 Corinthians 1:20 MSG

FOR THE CLASS OF
2014

Know the true value of time; snatch, seize, and enjoy every moment of it. No idleness, no laziness, no procrastination: never put off till tomorrow what you can do today.

—Lord Chesterfield

Don't waste your time on useless work, mere busywork, the barren pursuits of darkness. Expose these things for the sham they are.

Ephesians 5:11 MSG

FOR THE CLASS OF
2014

No person has the right to rain on your dreams.

—*Marian Wright Edelman*

I can do all things through Christ who strengthens me.

Philippians 4:13 NKJV

FOR THE CLASS OF
2014

We have a God who delights in impossibilities.

—*Andrew Murray*

Jesus replied, "What is impossible with man is possible with God."

Luke 18:27

GOD'S LITTLE

★ INSTRUCTION BOOK ★

You can give without loving, but you
cannot love without giving.

—Amy Carmichael

It is more blessed to give than to receive.

Acts 20:35

FOR THE CLASS OF
2014

Peace cannot be achieved through violence, it can only be attained through understanding.

—*Ralph Waldo Emerson*

Blessed are the peacemakers, for they will be called children of God.

Matthew 5:9

FOR THE CLASS OF
2014

Obedience is an act of faith; disobedience
is the result of unbelief.

—*Edwin Louis Cole*

**As obedient children, do not conform to the evil desires
you had when you lived in ignorance.**

1 Peter 1:14

FOR THE CLASS OF
2014

Snuggle in God's arms. When you are hurting, when you feel lonely, left out, let Him cradle you, comfort you, reassure you of His all-sufficient power and love.

—*Kay Arthur*

Let, I pray, Your merciful kindness be for my comfort.

Psalm 119:76 NKJV

FOR THE CLASS OF

2014

GOD'S LITTLE
★ INSTRUCTION BOOK ★

At the height of laughter, the universe is flung
into a kaleidoscope of new possibilities.

—*Jean Houston*

**He will yet fill your mouth with laughter and your lips with
shouts of joy.**

Job 8:21

FOR THE CLASS OF
2014

The future belongs to those who see
possibilities before they become obvious.

—*John Sculley*

Now listen, you who say, "Today or tomorrow we will go to
this or that city, spend a year there, carry on business and
make money." Why, you do not even know what will happen
tomorrow. What is your life? You are a mist that appears for
a little while and then vanishes. Instead, you ought to say, "If
it is the Lord's will, we will live and do this or that."

James 4:13–15

FOR THE CLASS OF

2014

Luck is a matter of preparation meeting opportunity.

—*Oprah Winfrey*

Make the most of every opportunity.

Colossians 4:5

FOR THE CLASS OF

2014

We never test the resources of God until
we attempt the impossible.

—*F. B. Meyer*

**Now faith is confidence in what we hope for and
assurance about what we do not see.**

Hebrews 11:1

FOR THE CLASS OF
2014

GOD'S LITTLE

★ INSTRUCTION BOOK ★

To believe in God is to know that all the rules will be fair, and that there will be wonderful surprises!

—Corita Kent

God is not unjust; he will not forget your work and the love you have shown him.

Hebrews 6:10

FOR THE CLASS OF

2014

Problems are not stop signs, they are guidelines.

—Robert H. Schuller

When the way is rough, your patience has a chance to grow. So let it grow, and don't try to squirm out of your problems.

James 1:3-4 TLB

FOR THE CLASS OF
2014

GOD'S LITTLE

★ INSTRUCTION BOOK ★

When you do the things you need to do when you need to do them, the day will come when you can do the things you want to do when you want to do them.

—Zig Ziglar

And keep the charge of the Lord your God, walking in his ways and keeping his statutes, his commandments, his rules, and his testimonies, as it is written in the Law of Moses, that you may prosper in all that you do and wherever you turn.

1 Kings 2:3 ESV

FOR THE CLASS OF

A good head and a good heart are always a formidable combination.

—*Nelson Mandela*

For wisdom will enter your heart, and knowledge will fill you with joy.

Proverbs 2:10 NLT

The most valuable possession you can own
is an open heart. The most powerful weapon
you can be is an instrument of peace.

—*Carlos Santana*

**I am leaving you with a gift—peace of mind and heart!
And the peace I give isn't fragile like the peace the world
gives. So don't be troubled or afraid.**

John 14:27 TLB

FOR THE CLASS OF
2014

If you're trying to achieve, there will be roadblocks. I've had them; everybody has had them. But obstacles don't have to stop you. If you run into a wall, don't turn around and give up. Figure out how to climb it, go through it, or work around it.

—*Michael Jordan*

Let us throw off everything that hinders and the sin that so easily entangles. And let us run with perseverance the race marked out for us.

Hebrews 12:1

FOR THE CLASS OF

GOD'S LITTLE
★INSTRUCTION BOOK★

Always do right. This will gratify some
people, and astonish the rest.

—Mark Twain

**This is a trustworthy saying, and I want you to insist on
these teachings so that all who trust in God will devote
themselves to doing good. These teachings are good and
beneficial for everyone.**

Titus 3:8 NLT

FOR THE CLASS OF

All life demands struggle. Those who have everything given to them become lazy, selfish, and insensitive to the real values of life. The very striving and hard work that we so constantly try to avoid is the major building block in the person we are today.

—*Pope Paul VI*

For we are God's handiwork, created in Christ Jesus to do good works, which God prepared in advance for us to do.

Ephesians 2:10

FOR THE CLASS OF
2014

GOD'S LITTLE
★ **INSTRUCTION BOOK** ★

It's not hard to make decisions when
you know what your values are.

—*Roy Disney*

Daniel purposed in his heart that he would not defile himself.

Daniel 1:8 KJV

FOR THE CLASS OF
2014

I would rather fail in the cause that someday will triumph than triumph in a cause that someday will fail.

—*Woodrow Wilson*

Thanks be to God who always leads us in triumph in Christ.

2 Corinthians 2:14 NKJV

FOR THE CLASS OF
2014

GOD'S LITTLE
★ **INSTRUCTION BOOK** ★

There is only one secure foundation: a genuine, deep relationship with Jesus Christ, which will carry you through any and all turmoil. No matter what storms are raging all around, you'll stand firm if you stand on His love.

—*Charles Stanley*

Christ's love compels us, because we are convinced that one died for all.

2 Corinthians 5:14

FOR THE CLASS OF
2014

My faith isn't in the idea that I'm more moral than anybody else. My faith is in the idea that God and His love are greater than whatever sins any of us commit.

—*Rich Mullins*

I sought the LORD**, and he answered me; he delivered me from all my fears.**

Psalm 34:4

A true friend never gets in your way unless
you happen to be going down.

—*Arnold Glasow*

**If either of them falls down, one can help the other up. But
pity anyone who falls and has no one to help them up.**

Ecclesiastes 4:10

FOR THE CLASS OF
2014

Obedience to the call of Christ nearly always costs everything to two people: the one who is called, and the one who loves that one.

—*Oswald Chambers*

If you will indeed obey My voice and keep My covenant, then you shall be a special treasure to Me above all people; for all the earth is Mine.

Exodus 19:5 NKJV

FOR THE CLASS OF

GOD'S LITTLE
★ INSTRUCTION BOOK ★

I am determined to be cheerful and happy in whatever situation I may find myself. For I have learned that the greater part of our misery or unhappiness is determined not by our circumstance but by our disposition.

—Martha Washington

A cheerful disposition is good for your health; gloom and doom leave you bone-tired.

Proverbs 17:22 MSG

FOR THE CLASS OF
2014

Whatever you dislike in another person,
take care to correct in yourself.

—*Thomas Sprat*

Why do you look at the speck of sawdust in your brother's eye and pay no attention to the plank in your own eye?

Matthew 7:3

FOR THE CLASS OF
2014

GOD'S LITTLE
★ **INSTRUCTION BOOK** ★

I count him braver who overcomes his desires than him who conquers his enemies; for the hardest victory is the victory over self.

—Aristotle

For God has not given us a spirit of fear and timidity, but of power, love, and self-discipline.

2 Timothy 1:7 NLT

FOR THE CLASS OF
2014

Trust in yourself and you are doomed to disappointment; ... but trust in God, and you are never to be confounded in time or eternity.

—*Dwight L. Moody*

Trust in the LORD with all your heart and lean not on your own understanding.

Proverbs 3:5

FOR THE CLASS OF
2014

GOD'S LITTLE
★ INSTRUCTION BOOK ★

A knowledge of the Bible without a college course is more valuable than a college course without the Bible.

—*William Lyon Phelps*

All scripture is given by inspiration of God, and is profitable for doctrine, for reproof, for correction, for instruction in righteousness: That the man of God may be perfect, thoroughly furnished unto all good works.

2 Timothy 3:16–17 KJV

FOR THE CLASS OF
2014

Never be afraid to trust an unknown future to a known God.

—*Corrie ten Boom*

I will turn the darkness into light before them and make the rough places smooth.

Isaiah 42:16

FOR THE CLASS OF
2014

Success consists of getting up just
one more time than you fall.

—*Oliver Goldsmith*

**For the righteous falls seven times and rises again, but the
wicked stumble in times of calamity.**

Proverbs 24:16 ESV

FOR THE CLASS OF
2014

You are only what you are when no one is looking.

—*Robert C. Edwards*

Not by way of eyeservice, as men-pleasers, but as slaves of Christ, doing the will of God from the heart.

Ephesians 6:6 NASB

FOR THE CLASS OF

GOD'S LITTLE

★INSTRUCTION BOOK★

God gave us the gift of life; it is up to us to
give ourselves the gift of living well.

—*Voltaire*

I have come that they may have life, and have it to the full.

John 10:10

FOR THE CLASS OF

Little minds are tamed and subdued by misfortune; but great minds rise above it.

—*Washington Irving*

Consider it pure joy, my brothers and sisters, whenever you face trials of many kinds.

James 1:2

FOR THE CLASS OF
2014

Perseverance is a great element of success. If you only knock long enough and loud enough at the gate, you are sure to wake up somebody.

—*Henry Wadsworth Longfellow*

Ask and it will be given to you; seek and you will find; knock and the door will be opened to you.

Luke 11:9

FOR THE CLASS OF
2014

Do not seek to follow in the footsteps of the men of old; seek what they sought.

—*Matsuo Basho*

I love everyone who loves me, and I will be found by all who honestly search.

Proverbs 8:17 CEV

GOD'S LITTLE
★ INSTRUCTION BOOK ★

One of Life's great rules is this: The more
you give, the more you get.

—William H. Danforth

**The generous will prosper; those who refresh others will
themselves be refreshed.**

Proverbs 11:25 NLT

FOR THE CLASS OF
2014

To trust in Him when no need is pressing, when things seem going right of themselves, may be harder than when things seem going wrong.

—George MacDonald

Give me neither poverty nor riches, but give me only my daily bread. Otherwise, I may have too much and disown you and say, "Who is the Lord?" Or I may become poor and steal, and so dishonor the name of my God.

Proverbs 30:8–9

FOR THE CLASS OF

2014

Shoot for the moon. Even if you miss,
you'll land among the stars.

—*Les Brown*

Be perfect.

2 Corinthians 13:11 KJV

FOR THE CLASS OF
2014

God is God. Because He is God, He is worthy of my trust and obedience. I will find rest nowhere but in His holy will, a will that is unspeakably beyond my largest notions of what He is up to.

—*Elisabeth Elliot*

It is better to take refuge in the LORD than to trust in humans.

Psalm 118:8

FOR THE CLASS OF
2014

GOD'S LITTLE
★ INSTRUCTION BOOK ★

I am only one, but still I am one. I cannot do everything, but still I can do something.... I will not refuse to do the something that I can do.

—*Edward Everett Hale*

Under [Christ's] direction the whole body is fitted together perfectly, and each part in its own special way helps the other parts.

Ephesians 4:16 TLB

FOR THE CLASS OF
2014

Anything I've ever done that ultimately was worthwhile initially scared me to death.

—*Betty Bender*

When I am afraid, I put my trust in you. In God, whose word I praise—in God I trust and am not afraid. What can mere mortals do to me?

Psalm 56:3–4

GOD'S LITTLE
★ INSTRUCTION BOOK ★

Never, never, never give up.

—*Winston Churchill*

As for you, brothers, do not grow weary in doing good.

2 Thessalonians 3:13 ESV

FOR THE CLASS OF

No matter what a man's past may have been, his future is spotless.

—*John R. Rice*

As far as the east is from the west, so far has he removed our transgressions from us.

Psalm 103:12

Do not borrow trouble by dreading tomorrow. It is the dark menace of the future that makes cowards of us all.

—*Dorothy Dix*

For he will order his angels to protect you wherever you go.

Psalm 91:11 NLT

FOR THE CLASS OF
2014

Remember not only to say the right thing in the right place, but far more difficult still, to leave unsaid the wrong thing at the tempting moment.

—*Benjamin Franklin*

Careful words make for a careful life; careless talk may ruin everything.

Proverbs 13:3 MSG

I think the one lesson I have learned is that there is no substitute for paying attention.

—*Diane Sawyer*

We must pay the most careful attention, therefore, to what we have heard, so that we do not drift away.

Hebrews 2:1

FOR THE CLASS OF
2014

Perfection is not attainable, but if we chase
perfection we can catch excellence.

—*Vince Lombardi*

**Daniel was preferred above the presidents and princes,
because an excellent spirit was in him.**

Daniel 6:3 KJV

FOR THE CLASS OF
2014

GOD'S LITTLE

★ **INSTRUCTION BOOK** ★

When we long for life without difficulties, remind
us that oaks grow strong in contrary winds
and diamonds are made under pressure.

—*Peter Marshall*

**But you must learn to endure everything, so that you will
be completely mature and not lacking in anything.**

James 1:4 CEV

FOR THE CLASS OF

2014

The happiest people don't necessarily have the best of everything. They just make the best of everything.

—*Author unknown*

I have learned the secret of being content in any and every situation.

Philippians 4:12

GOD'S LITTLE
★ INSTRUCTION BOOK ★

Blessed is the man who finds out which way God is moving and then gets going in the same direction.

—Author unknown

Whether you turn to the right or to the left, your ears will hear a voice behind you, saying, "This is the way; walk in it."

Isaiah 30:21

FOR THE CLASS OF

2014

Nothing is ever lost by courtesy.... It pleases him who gives and him who receives, and thus, like mercy, it is twice blessed.

—*Erastus Wiman*

While we have opportunity, let us do good to all people.

Galatians 6:10 NASB

Here's the key to success and the key to failure: we become what we think about.

—Earl Nightingale

Whatever is true, whatever is noble, whatever is right, whatever is pure, whatever is lovely, whatever is admirable—if anything is excellent or praiseworthy—think about such things.

Philippians 4:8

FOR THE CLASS OF
2014

Legalism says God will love us if we change. The gospel says God will change us because He loves us.

—*Tullian Tchividjian*

Being confident of this, that he who began a good work in you will carry it on to completion until the day of Christ Jesus.

Philippians 1:6

FOR THE CLASS OF

GOD'S LITTLE
★ INSTRUCTION BOOK ★

Though we are incomplete, God loves us completely.
Though we are imperfect, He loves us perfectly.
Though we may feel lost and without compass,
God's love encompasses us completely.

—Dieter F. Uchtdorf

For I am convinced that neither death nor life, neither angels nor demons, neither the present nor the future, nor any powers, neither height nor depth, nor anything else in all creation, will be able to separate us from the love of God that is in Christ Jesus our Lord.

Romans 8:38–39

FOR THE CLASS OF

Sainthood lies in the habit of referring
the smallest actions to God.

—*C. S. Lewis*

"Therefore I tell you, do not be anxious about your life, what you will eat or what you will drink, nor about your body, what you will put on. Is not life more than food, and the body more than clothing? Look at the birds of the air: they neither sow nor reap nor gather into barns, and yet your heavenly Father feeds them. Are you not of more value than they?"

Matthew 6:25–26 ESV

FOR THE CLASS OF

2014

GOD'S LITTLE
★ INSTRUCTION BOOK ★

I learned that courage was not the absence of fear, but the triumph over it. The brave man is not he who does not feel afraid, but he who conquers that fear.

—*Nelson Mandela*

Have not I commanded you? Be strong, vigorous, and very courageous. Be not afraid, neither be dismayed, for the Lord your God is with you wherever you go.

Joshua 1:9 AMP

FOR THE CLASS OF

You may be disappointed if you fail, but
you are doomed if you don't try.

—*Beverly Sills*

A sluggard's appetite is never filled, but the desires of the diligent are fully satisfied.

Proverbs 13:4

GOD'S LITTLE
★ INSTRUCTION BOOK ★

It's a good thing to have all the props pulled out from under us occasionally. It gives us some sense of what is rock under our feet, and what is sand.

—*Madeleine L'Engle*

He is the Rock, his works are perfect, and all his ways are just. A faithful God who does no wrong, upright and just is he.

Deuteronomy 32:4

FOR THE CLASS OF
2014

Real prayer comes not from gritting our
teeth but from falling in love.

—*Richard Foster*

**By day the Lord directs his love, at night his song is with
me—a prayer to the God of my life.**

Psalm 42:8

FOR THE CLASS OF
2014

GOD'S LITTLE
★ INSTRUCTION BOOK ★

Carve your name on hearts and not on marble.

—*Charles H. Spurgeon*

The only letter I need is you yourselves! ... They can see that you are a letter from Christ, written by us ... not one carved on stone, but in human hearts.

2 Corinthians 3:2–3 TLB

FOR THE CLASS OF

It is impossible for that man to despair who remembers that his Helper is omnipotent.

—*Jeremy Taylor*

I will lift up my eyes to the mountains; from where shall my help come? My help comes from the LORD, who made heaven and earth.

Psalm 121:1–2 NASB

FOR THE CLASS OF
2014

GOD'S LITTLE

★ INSTRUCTION BOOK ★

This world belongs to the man who is wise enough
to change his mind in the presence of facts.

—*Roy L. Smith*

The one who heeds correction gains understanding.

Proverbs 15:32

FOR THE CLASS OF
2014

Where fear is present, wisdom cannot be.

—*Lucius C. Lactantius*

The Lord is my light and my salvation—whom shall I fear?

Psalm 27:1

GOD'S LITTLE
★ INSTRUCTION BOOK ★

The world is governed more by appearance than realities.

—*Daniel Webster*

These are a shadow of the things that were to come; the reality, however, is found in Christ.

Colossians 2:17

FOR THE CLASS OF
2014

Never despair; but if you do, work on in despair.

—*Edmund Burke*

As for you, be strong and do not give up, for your work will be rewarded.

2 Chronicles 15:7

GOD'S LITTLE

★ INSTRUCTION BOOK ★

Most of the things worth doing in the world had
been declared impossible before they were done.

—*Louis D. Brandeis*

For nothing will be impossible with God.

Luke 1:37 ESV

FOR THE CLASS OF
2014

When you are laboring for others, let it be with
the same zeal as if it were for yourself.

—Confucius

**Put yourself aside, and help others get ahead. Don't
be obsessed with getting your own advantage. Forget
yourselves long enough to lend a helping hand.**

Philippians 2:4 MSG

FOR THE CLASS OF
2014

GOD'S LITTLE
★ INSTRUCTION BOOK ★

The most important single ingredient in the formula of success is knowing how to get along with people.

—*Theodore Roosevelt*

See that no one pays back evil for evil, but always try to do good to each other and to everyone else.

1 Thessalonians 5:15 TLB

FOR THE CLASS OF
2014

Life can only be understood backwards;
but it must be lived forwards.

—*Søren Kierkegaard*

This is what the Lord says—your Redeemer, the Holy One of Israel: "I am the Lord your God, who teaches you what is best for you, who directs you in the way you should go."

Isaiah 48:17

GOD'S LITTLE

★ INSTRUCTION BOOK ★

Success is never final; failure is never fatal. It is courage that counts.

—*Winston Churchill*

Be of good courage, and he shall strengthen your heart, all ye that hope in the LORD**.**

Psalm 31:24 KJV

FOR THE CLASS OF

2014

To love what you do and feel that it matters—
how could anything be more fun?

—*Katharine Graham*

For my heart rejoiced in all my labour.

Ecclesiastes 2:10 KJV

FOR THE CLASS OF

2014

GOD'S LITTLE
★ **INSTRUCTION BOOK** ★

Every calling is great when greatly pursued.

—*Oliver Wendell Holmes*

I press toward the mark for the prize of the high calling of God in Christ Jesus.

Philippians 3:14 KJV

FOR THE CLASS OF
2014

When you were born, you cried and the world rejoiced. Live your life in such a way that when you die, the world cries and you rejoice.

—*Indian proverb*

For to me, living means living for Christ, and dying is even better.

Philippians 1:21 NLT

FOR THE CLASS OF
2014

The secret of success is to do the common things uncommonly well.

—*John D. Rockefeller Jr.*

Do you see a man who excels in his work? He will stand before kings; he will not stand before unknown men.

Proverbs 22:29 NKJV

FOR THE CLASS OF
2014

The cheerful man will do more in the same time, will do it better, will preserve it longer, than the sad or sullen.

—*Thomas Carlyle*

When a man is gloomy, everything seems to go wrong; when he is cheerful, everything seems right!

Proverbs 15:15 TLB

FOR THE CLASS OF
2014

Only passions, great passions, can
elevate the soul to great things.

—*Denis Diderot*

Fervent in spirit; serving the Lord.

Romans 12:11 KJV

FOR THE CLASS OF

2014

The greater part of our happiness or misery depends on our disposition and not our circumstances.

—*Martha Washington*

I know how to live on almost nothing or with everything. I have learned the secret of contentment in every situation.

Philippians 4:12 TLB

FOR THE CLASS OF
2014

Don't be discouraged; everyone who got
where he is, started where he was.

—*Author unknown*

**Though your beginning was insignificant, yet your end will
increase greatly.**

Job 8:7 NASB

FOR THE CLASS OF
2014

Prayer is an invisible tool which is wielded in a visible world.

—Ed Cole

The weapons of our warfare are not carnal, but mighty through God to the pulling down of strong holds.

2 Corinthians 10:4 KJV

FOR THE CLASS OF
2014

GOD'S LITTLE

★ INSTRUCTION BOOK ★

Perseverance is the hard work you do after you get
tired of doing the hard work you already did.

—*Newt Gingrich*

**Let us not become weary in doing good, for at the proper
time we will reap a harvest if we do not give up.**

Galatians 6:9

FOR THE CLASS OF

2014

It is amidst great perils we see brave hearts.

—*Jean-François Regnard*

Then I'm up again—rested, tall and steady, fearless before the enemy mobs coming at me from all sides.

Psalm 3:6 MSG

GOD'S LITTLE

★ INSTRUCTION BOOK ★

An error doesn't become a mistake
until you refuse to correct it.

—Orlando A. Battista

**Whoever heeds discipline shows the way to life, but
whoever ignores correction leads others astray.**

Proverbs 10:17

FOR THE CLASS OF
2014

GOD'S LITTLE
★ INSTRUCTION BOOK ★

Hating people is like burning down your
own house to get rid of a rat.

—*Harry Emerson Fosdick*

**If you are always biting and devouring one another, watch
out! Beware of destroying one another.**

Galatians 5:15 NLT

FOR THE CLASS OF
2014

GOD'S LITTLE
★ INSTRUCTION BOOK ★

When you flee temptations, don't
leave a forwarding address.

—*Author unknown*

**Now flee from youthful lusts and pursue righteousness ...
with those who call on the Lord from a pure heart.**

2 Timothy 2:22 NASB

FOR THE CLASS OF
2014

We live in deeds, not years; in thoughts, not breaths....
We should count time by heart-throbs. He most lives
who thinks most, feels the noblest, acts the best.

—Philip James Bailey

**"For in him we live and move and have our being." As
some of your own poets have said, "We are his offspring."**

Acts 17:28

FOR THE CLASS OF
2014

Good nature begets smiles, smiles beget friends,
and friends are better than a fortune.

—Author unknown

The light in the eyes [of him whose heart is joyful] rejoices the hearts of others.

Proverbs 15:30 AMP

Children who bring honor to their parents
reap blessings from their God.

—Author unknown

**Honor your father and your mother, so that you may live
long in the land the LORD your God is giving you.**

Exodus 20:12

FOR THE CLASS OF
2014

GOD'S LITTLE
★ INSTRUCTION BOOK ★

Laughter is the sun which drives
winter from the human face.

—Victor Hugo

**A merry heart maketh a cheerful countenance: but by
sorrow of the heart the spirit is broken.**

Proverbs 15:13 KJV

FOR THE CLASS OF
2014

A good reputation is more valuable than money.

—*Publilius Syrus*

A good name is rather to be chosen than great riches.

Proverbs 22:1 KJV

FOR THE CLASS OF
2014

I don't know the secret to success, but the key
to failure is trying to please everybody.

—*Bill Cosby*

**Am I now trying to win the approval of human beings, or
of God?**

Galatians 1:10

FOR THE CLASS OF
2014

The Bible has a word to describe "safe"
sex: It's called marriage.

—*Gary Smalley & John Trent*

**Honor marriage, and guard the sacredness of sexual
intimacy between wife and husband. God draws a firm line
against casual and illicit sex.**

Hebrews 13:4 MSG

FOR THE CLASS OF
2014

GOD'S LITTLE
★ **INSTRUCTION BOOK** ★

Every charitable act is a stepping stone toward heaven.

—*Henry Ward Beecher*

Store your treasures in heaven, where moths and rust cannot destroy, and thieves do not break in and steal.

Matthew 6:20 NLT

FOR THE CLASS OF
2014

Never be in a hurry; do everything quietly and in a calm spirit. Do not lose your inner peace for anything whatsoever, even if your whole world seems upset.

—Saint Francis de Sales

A hot-tempered person stirs up conflict, but the one who is patient calms a quarrel.

Proverbs 15:18

FOR THE CLASS OF

2014

GOD'S LITTLE
★ INSTRUCTION BOOK ★

God has wisely kept us in the dark concerning future events, and reserved to Himself the knowledge of them ... that He may train us up in a dependence upon Himself, and a continued readiness for every event.

—*Matthew Henry*

The vision is yet for an appointed time ... it will surely come, it will not tarry.

Habakkuk 2:3 KJV

FOR THE CLASS OF
2014

The mind grows by what it feeds on.

—J. G. Holland

The mind governed by the Spirit is life and peace.

Romans 8:6

FOR THE CLASS OF
2014

All our dreams can come true, if we have
the courage to pursue them.

—Walt Disney

**Be strong and courageous. Do not be afraid or terrified
because of them, for the Lord your God goes with you; he
will never leave you nor forsake you.**

Deuteronomy 31:6

FOR THE CLASS OF
2014

Vision is the world's most desperate need. There are no hopeless situations, only people who think hopelessly.

—*Winifred Newman*

Where there is no vision, the people perish.

Proverbs 29:18 KJV

FOR THE CLASS OF

GOD'S LITTLE

★INSTRUCTION BOOK★

Once a word has been allowed to
escape, it cannot be recalled.

—Horace

**Do not let any unwholesome talk come out of your
mouths, but only what is helpful for building others up
according to their needs, that it may benefit those who
listen.**

Ephesians 4:29

FOR THE CLASS OF

It often happens that those of whom we speak least on earth are best known in heaven.

—*Nicolas Caussin*

You are the ones chosen by God, chosen for the high calling of priestly work, chosen to be a holy people, God's instruments to do his work and speak out for him.

1 Peter 2:9 MSG

GOD'S LITTLE
★ INSTRUCTION BOOK ★

Motivation is when your dreams put on work clothes.

—*Benjamin Franklin*

Whatever you do, work at it with all your heart, as working for the Lord, not for human masters.

Colossians 3:23

FOR THE CLASS OF
2014

A good listener is not only popular everywhere,
but after a while he gets to know something.

—*Wilson Mizner*

The ear that hears the rebukes of life will abide among the wise.

Proverbs 15:31 NKJV

FOR THE CLASS OF
2014

The capacity to care ... gives life its deepest meaning and significance.

—*Pablo Casals*

Bear one another's burdens, and thereby fulfill the law of Christ.

Galatians 6:2 NASB

FOR THE CLASS OF
2014

The only way to have a friend is to be one.

—*Ralph Waldo Emerson*

A man that hath friends must [show] himself friendly.

Proverbs 18:24 KJV

It is presumptuous in me to wish to choose my path, because I cannot tell which path is best for me. I must leave it to the Lord, who knows me, to lead me by the path which is best for me, so that in all things His will may be done.

—*Teresa of Ávila*

In peace I will lie down and sleep, for you alone, O LORD, will keep me safe.

Psalm 4:8 NLT

FOR THE CLASS OF

2014

The future belongs to those who believe
in the beauty of their dreams.

—Eleanor Roosevelt

"Anything is possible if you have faith."

Mark 9:23 TLB

GOD'S LITTLE

★ INSTRUCTION BOOK ★

God takes life's pieces and gives us unbroken peace.

—W. D. Gough

The peace of God, which surpasses all understanding, will guard your hearts and minds through Christ Jesus.

Philippians 4:7 NKJV

FOR THE CLASS OF

2014

Jumping to conclusions is not half as good
an exercise as digging for facts.

—*Author unknown*

**Do your best to present yourself to God as one approved,
a worker who does not need to be ashamed and who
correctly handles the word of truth.**

2 Timothy 2:15

GOD'S LITTLE
★ INSTRUCTION BOOK ★

He who created us without our help will
not save us without our consent.

—St. Augustine

If you confess with your mouth, "Jesus is Lord," and believe in your heart that God raised him from the dead, you will be saved.

Romans 10:9

FOR THE CLASS OF
2014

You can accomplish more in one hour with
God than one lifetime without Him.

—Author unknown

With God all things are possible.

Matthew 19:26 KJV

To be a Christian means to forgive the inexcusable because God has forgiven the inexcusable in you.

—*C. S. Lewis*

But when you are praying, first forgive anyone you are holding a grudge against, so that your Father in heaven will forgive your sins, too.

Mark 11:25 NLT

FOR THE CLASS OF
2014

School seeks to get you ready for examination; life gives the finals.

—*Anonymous*

Examine yourselves to see whether you are in the faith; test yourselves.

2 Corinthians 13:5

GOD'S LITTLE
★ INSTRUCTION BOOK ★

Within your heart
Keep one still, secret spot
Where dreams may go,
And, sheltered so,
May thrive and grow.

—*Louise Driscoll*

Above all else, guard your heart, for everything you do flows from it.

Proverbs 4:23

FOR THE CLASS OF
2014

Family is not an important thing. It's everything.

—*Michael J. Fox*

You should be like one big happy family ... loving one another with tender hearts and humble minds.

1 Peter 3:8 TLB

FOR THE CLASS OF
2014

GOD'S LITTLE

★ INSTRUCTION BOOK ★

There is no poverty that can overtake diligence.

—*Japanese proverb*

Sloth makes you poor; diligence brings wealth.

Proverbs 10:4 MSG

FOR THE CLASS OF

2014

Many receive advice; only the wise profit by it.

—*Publilius Syrus*

Where there is strife, there is pride, but wisdom is found in those who take advice.

Proverbs 13:10

Opportunities are seldom labeled.

—*John A. Shedd*

Seek, and ye shall find; knock, and it shall be opened unto you.

Matthew 7:7 KJV

FOR THE CLASS OF
2014

Unless you try to do something beyond what you have already mastered, you will never grow.

—*Ronald E. Osborn*

Brethren, I do not regard myself as having laid hold of it yet; but one thing I do: forgetting what lies behind and reaching forward to what lies ahead, I press on toward the goal for the prize of the upward call of God in Christ Jesus.

Philippians 3:13–14 NASB

FOR THE CLASS OF

2014

GOD'S LITTLE
★ INSTRUCTION BOOK ★

Before you borrow money from a friend,
decide which you need more.

—Author unknown

If anyone borrows an animal from their neighbor and it is injured or dies while the owner is not present, they must make restitution.

Exodus 22:14

FOR THE CLASS OF
2014

Never fear shadows. They simply mean there's a light shining somewhere nearby.

—Ruth E. Renkel

Yea, though I walk through the valley of the shadow of death, I will fear no evil: for thou art with me.

Psalm 23:4 KJV

FOR THE CLASS OF

2014

GOD'S LITTLE
★ INSTRUCTION BOOK ★

Let us not say, "Every man is the architect of his own fortune," but let us say, "Every man is the architect of his own character."

—*George Dana Boardman*

I will defend my integrity until I die. I will maintain my innocence without wavering. My conscience is clear for as long as I live.

Job 27:5-6 NLT

FOR THE CLASS OF
2014

Obstacles are those frightful things you see
when you take your eyes off your goal.

—*Henry Ford*

We know that in all things God works for the good of those who love him, who have been called according to his purpose.

Romans 8:28

FOR THE CLASS OF
2014

GOD'S LITTLE

★ INSTRUCTION BOOK ★

The Bible knows nothing of a hierarchy of labor. No work is degrading. If it ought to be done, then it is good work.

—Author unknown

To rejoice in his labour; this is the gift of God.

Ecclesiastes 5:19 KJV

FOR THE CLASS OF
2014

'Tis better to be alone than in bad company.

—*George Washington*

Do not be misled: "Bad company corrupts good character."

1 Corinthians 15:33

FOR THE CLASS OF
2014

GOD'S LITTLE

★ INSTRUCTION BOOK ★

I like the dreams of the future better
than the history of the past.

—*Thomas Jefferson*

**Forget about what's happened; don't keep going over old
history. Be alert, be present. I'm about to do something
brand-new. It's bursting out! Don't you see it?**

Isaiah 43:18–19 MSG

You can lead a boy to college, but
you cannot make him think.

—*Kin Hubbard*

It is senseless to pay tuition to educate a rebel who has no heart for truth.

Proverbs 17:16 TLB

FOR THE CLASS OF
2014

GOD'S LITTLE

★ INSTRUCTION BOOK ★

Unless we form the habit of going to the Bible in bright moments as well as in trouble, we cannot fully respond to its consolations because we lack equilibrium between light and darkness.

—*Helen Keller*

No discipline is enjoyable while it is happening—it's painful! But afterward there will be a peaceful harvest of right living for those who are trained in this way.

Hebrews 12:11 NLT

FOR THE CLASS OF

God never put anyone in a place too small to grow in.

—Author unknown

Give thanks in all circumstances, for this is God's will for you in Christ Jesus.

1 Thessalonians 5:18

FOR THE CLASS OF
2014

GOD'S LITTLE
★ **INSTRUCTION BOOK** ★

Maturity: Be able to stick with a job until it is finished.
Be able to bear an injustice without having to get
even. Be able to carry money without spending
it. Do your duty without being supervised.

—Ann Landers

**When I was a child, I spoke as a child, I understood as a
child, I thought as a child; but when I became a man, I put
away childish things.**

1 Corinthians 13:11 NKJV

FOR THE CLASS OF

You must have long-range goals to keep you from being frustrated by short-range failures.

—*Charles C. Noble*

Fix our eyes on Jesus, the pioneer and perfecter of faith. For the joy set before him he endured the cross, scorning its shame, and sat down at the right hand of the throne of God.

Hebrews 12:2

FOR THE CLASS OF
2014

Many men have too much willpower.
It's won't power they lack.

—*Author unknown*

A man without self-control is as defenseless as a city with broken-down walls.

Proverbs 25:28 TLB

FOR THE CLASS OF
2014

Politeness goes far, yet costs nothing.

—*Samuel Smiles*

Those who are kind benefit themselves.

Proverbs 11:17

GOD'S LITTLE
★ INSTRUCTION BOOK ★

Keep your fears to yourself, but share
your inspiration with others.

—*Robert Louis Stevenson*

**Honor Christ and let him be the Lord of your life. Always
be ready to give an answer when someone asks you about
your hope.**

1 Peter 3:15 CEV

FOR THE CLASS OF

Life is a coin. You can spend it any way you wish, but you can spend it only once.

—*Lillian Dickson*

It is appointed unto men once to die, but after this the judgment.

Hebrews 9:27 KJV

FOR THE CLASS OF
2014

Truth, like surgery, may hurt, but it cures.

—*Han Suyin*

Speaking the truth in love, we will grow to become in every respect the mature body of him who is the head, that is, Christ.

Ephesians 4:15

FOR THE CLASS OF

2014

Don't count on your education to make you wise.

—Author unknown

Those who trust in themselves are fools, but those who walk in wisdom are kept safe.

Proverbs 28:26

FOR THE CLASS OF
2014

GOD'S LITTLE
★ INSTRUCTION BOOK ★

Most of the verses written about praise in God's Word were voiced by people who were faced with crushing heartaches, injustice, treachery, slander, and scores of other difficult situations.

—Joni Eareckson Tada

David sang to the LORD ... when the LORD delivered him from the hand of all his enemies.... He said: "The LORD is my rock, my fortress and my deliverer."

2 Samuel 22:1–2

FOR THE CLASS OF

We too often love things and use people, when we should be using things and loving people.

—*Author unknown*

Love each other with genuine affection, and take delight in honoring each other.

Romans 12:10 NLT

FOR THE CLASS OF
2014

GOD'S LITTLE
★ **INSTRUCTION BOOK** ★

You can't test courage cautiously.

—*Annie Dillard*

So do not fear, for I am with you; do not be dismayed, for I am your God. I will strengthen you and help you; I will uphold you with my righteous right hand.

Isaiah 41:10

FOR THE CLASS OF

2014

I believe God is managing affairs and that He doesn't need any advice from me. With God in charge, I believe everything will work out for the best in the end. So what is there to worry about.

—*Henry Ford*

My help comes from the Lord, the Maker of heaven and earth.

Psalm 121:2

FOR THE CLASS OF
2014

GOD'S LITTLE

★ INSTRUCTION BOOK ★

I have also decided to stick with love....
Hate is too great a burden to bear.

—Martin Luther King Jr.

Do everything in love.

1 Corinthians 16:14

To believe in something, and not to live it, is dishonest.

—*Mahatma Gandhi*

If we live by the Spirit, let us also walk by the Spirit.

Galatians 5:25 NASB

FOR THE CLASS OF
2014

GOD'S LITTLE

★ INSTRUCTION BOOK ★

Some debts are fun when you are acquiring them, but none are fun when you set about retiring them.

—*Ogden Nash*

Why do you spend money for what is not bread, and your wages for what does not satisfy? Listen carefully to Me, and eat what is good, and delight yourself in abundance.

Isaiah 55:2 NASB

FOR THE CLASS OF

2014

In His will is our peace.

—*Dante Alighieri*

Great peace have those who love Your law, and nothing causes them to stumble.

Psalm 119:165 NKJV

GOD'S LITTLE
★ INSTRUCTION BOOK ★

Diligence is the mother of good fortune.

—Cervantes

The plans of the diligent lead to profit.

Proverbs 21:5

FOR THE CLASS OF
2014

I am convinced that faith sometimes means knowing God can, whether or not He does.

—Beth Moore

The God we worship can save us from you and your flaming furnace. But even if he doesn't, we still won't worship your gods and the gold statue you have set up.

Daniel 3:17–18 CEV

FOR THE CLASS OF

2014

GOD'S LITTLE

★ INSTRUCTION BOOK ★

Let your words be the genuine picture of your heart.

—*John Wesley*

My mouth shall speak wisdom, and the meditation of my heart shall give understanding.

Psalm 49:3 NKJV

FOR THE CLASS OF

2014

Call on God, but row away from the rocks.

—*Hunter S. Thompson*

Wisdom and good judgment live together, for wisdom knows where to discover knowledge and understanding.

Proverbs 8:12 TLB

FOR THE CLASS OF
2014

GOD'S LITTLE

★ INSTRUCTION BOOK ★

We need to pay more attention to how we
treat people than to how they treat us.

—*Joyce Meyers*

Love others as well as you love yourself.

Mark 12:31 MSG

FOR THE CLASS OF
2014

Go confidently in the direction of your dreams. Live the life you have imagined.

—*Henry David Thoreau*

"For I know the plans I have for you," declares the Lord, "plans to prosper you and not to harm you, plans to give you hope and a future."

Jeremiah 29:11

FOR THE CLASS OF
2014